KISSING THE BEE

Lara Gularte

The Bitter Oleander Press
4983 Tall Oaks Drive
Fayetteville, New York 13066-9776
USA

www.bitteroleander.com
info@bitteroleander.com

ISBN #: 978-0-9862049-7-5

Library of Congress Control Number: 2017955982

Cover Design: Roderick Martinez

Printed by McNaughton & Gunn, Inc.
Saline, Michigan 48176-0010
www.bookprinters.com

Distributed in the United States by
Small Press Distribution, Inc.
Berkeley, CA 94710-1409
www.spdbooks.org

Manufactured in the United States of America

ACKNOWLEDGMENTS

I wish to express special gratitude to Frank X. Gaspar, who edited an earlier version of this manuscript. I am also indebted to Paul B. Roth for his artistic support and who I consider both a mentor and friend. Thank you, Red Fox Poets of the Sierra foothills for Sunday morning poetry and to Calder Lowe, editor of *Dragonfly Press*, for her generosity and faith in my words. I would like to thank Footpaths to Creativity Center an Artist/Writer Residency on Flores Island where some of these poems were written. I must also give credit to Al Young, Lucille Clifton, Alan Soldofsky, and Vamberto Freitas for encouraging and promoting my work.

Also, grateful acknowledgment is made to the following publications in which poems from this collection first appeared, sometimes in a slightly different form:

The Bitter Oleander: "A One Breasted Woman Dressed in a Shroud," "Mrs. Madruga Prepares Her Granddaughter for Hard Times," "The Old Woman's Last Days," "Transparent Sphere," "Soul of Black Stone," "Penance," "A Seashell Mythology," "Bone Hunting in the Sierras," "In the Woods at Night," "The Surge," "She Enters an Inuit World," "Crow Crossing," "The Pull of Water," "Flores Island," "Dreaming Vulcan," "What the Tide Brings In," "Hanging On," "Approaching the Last Season," "The Bird Inside Her Head," "Witch of Flores Island," "Woman of the Rowan," "Don't Scorn the Dead Who are Ourselves"

The Call: An Anthology of Women's Writing: "Saving Myself"

Caesura: "The Ghost of Mary Prada"

The Cape Rock: "Kissing the Bee"

Comunidades: "The Rancher's Wife"

The Monserrat Review: "Peach Canning"

Empirical Magazine: "Let Her Be a Flower"

The Gavea-Brown Book of Portuguese American Poetry: "What Matters in the Morning"

Kaleidoscope: "The Widow Silva"

The Manzanita Quarterly: "Uncle Ernie Tries to Shoot Me a Pet Bird"

Neo: "Festo do Emigrante; Flores Island"

Permafrost: "High Winds"

SAAL-Suplemento Acoriano de Artes e Letras, da revista Saber/Acores: "Looking for my great, great grandmother, Maria Francesca do Cabral"

The Santa Clara Review: "Crossing Over"

San Jose Mercury News, Gold Rush Series: "California Bride," "Mt. Shasta 1895: Great Aunt Lila and Her Husband Joe"

Sisters Singing Anthology: "Grandfather"

A Bird Black As The Sun, California Poets on Crows and Ravens: "Finding the Sacred"

Watershed: "In the Stars," "The Crossing," "Last of Her Line;" "Poppy Seeds on Stones"

Writers of the Portuguese Diaspora in the United States and Canada: An Anthology: "Bound," "The White City," "Lost Currents"

Zambomba: "Aunt Lucy."

Tiger's Eye, A Journal of Poetry: "Coiled Spring"

Windfall, A Journal of Poetry of Place: "Pray, Sing," "Fisherman at Eagle Lake, California"

Eclipse, A Literary Journal: "Mushroom Woods"

Lost Hills Press, Fog and Woodsmoke Anthology: "River in the Road"

Water-Stone Review: "Mercado"

Art/Life Magazine: "California Turning"

The Sand Hill Review: "Quercus," "Peach Canning"

Caesura, The End of the World Anthology: "Folklore"

Dragonfly Press, DNA EZINE: "Assumption," "The Shape of Grief"

Portuguese Heritage Publications of California: "Festa do Espirito Santo"

CONTENTS

PART ONE

PART TWO

PART THREE

KISSING THE BEE

For Brian, my partner in all life's escapades

Halfway to a House

I take light from the closet drawers. The first day
of fall. And all those years at the bottom.
Before, it wasn't me. It was a house under construction.
I before myself. Now I dismantle the summer,
dresses flying, naked feet beside a dress.
Time loses itself in the change of the seasons,
but in this loss someone exists in me.
A voice laughs deep within the closet.
The sun so low, in the bottom drawer.

—Rosa Alice Branco

PART ONE

All these seated strangers
my relations? I don't believe it.
They're guests amusing themselves
in a rarely-opened parlor.

—Carlos Drummond De Andrade

HANGING ON

The house leans toward the road.
She waits for someone to open the door
to the place where her mother was born.
No one at the window waves.

The old homestead settles in her chest.
This is where they lived,
set boundary fences, planted posts.
The well dry now, the creek diverted.
Clouds darken her memories.

She remembers where the oak tree stood,
tugs at the stump,
pulls on long roots and dank echoes.

With seeds in her pockets,
she smells the hope of rain,
and counts the seconds
between lightning and thunder,
distance narrowing.

Light strikes her and splits a sudden sky.
Rain flows through a hole inside herself,
memory glitters into clarity.

CALIFORNIA BRIDE

Bones half-grown, she rises
from a ship's dark hold.
Gives herself up
to a hard-handed miner,
grows thin from miscarriage,
fat from pregnancy.
Sings songs in Portuguese
as she hurries from cabin to sluice box
on small calloused feet.

I remember the old woman,
not the girl.
A widow in black,
with thick stockings, heavy shoes.
Lived in the corner
of my grandmother's kitchen
gluing broken dishes.
Always moving and praying.
Boiled her own egg
till the day she died.

The face of Maria Neves,
I wear her eyes,
speak in her voice.
She is waving her hands,
reshaping the air
to tell me in broken English,
that "life is no sugar."

MT. SHASTA 1895: GREAT AUNT LILA AND HER HUSBAND JOE

Lila and Joe homestead some land.
They fill a cabin and build a barn.
He is bow-legged, square-jawed,
cuts trees to earn a wage.
She waits for him wide-eyed,
at the kitchen table.
The stew grows cold,
the bread turns hard.
She thinks she hears a tree cry,
listens for the swish of a crosscut,
the snap and the shudder.

Through thistle and weeds,
down a muddy path,
her thin voice calls his name.
She finds him among rusty ferns,
face down, with no breath.
Covering him with her body,
she dreams the sun will climb
to the top of the mountain,
dreams he will come back,
lift her once again,
like a bride.

THE GHOST OF MARY PRADA

1

I come from an island of stones
to marry Joe.
In Pico,
stones on top of the land, underneath it
overflowing into the ocean.
With bare hands I claw through stones
to find the earth.

2

At my wedding I dance the Chamarita
with Joe.
A glass of red wine, then another,
my shawl, a heap on the floor.
We sleep good on an iron bed
with a big mattress.

3

Here in California I pluck cherries, apricots,
and prunes loose from limbs,
the sound of fruit striking the bottoms of buckets.
I grow vegetables:
Beet hearts, potatoes curled like pale grubs.
I milk cows, churn butter,
can fruits in tin cans sealed with wax.
I make soups of kale or cabbage,

a shriveled onion, a dried bean.
I pound dough into loaves.
Big with a baby,
I sit in the evening with my crocheting,
and I let the orchard come through the window.

4

When my boy breaks through me
blue and silent,
a stain seeps
red and sticky on the sheets.
The midwife bends over me,
dips a towel into a bucket of hot water.
Lying on my side, I can see out the window
the apple trees stretch over the hill.
A priest mumbles the rosary,
my Joe stares above me,
his hands at his sides, big and useless.

MRS. MADRUGA PREPARES HER GRANDDAUGHTER FOR HARD TIMES

Mrs. Madruga warns her granddaughter about the blurry sun, heavy and hungry, the scarred vegetables, the ragged turnips, and how the garden understands the natural cycle, the quiet of slaughter. She shows her granddaughter where to place the snares, to listen for the chuff of breath, how to get tender meat by relaxing the animal, stroking it from breastbone to pelvis till it slumps in her arms. She teaches her granddaughter how to kill, fast, painless, with the edge of an open hand striking a blow to the bones linking back to head; the snapped neck. She guides the chore of pulling out the shivering insides, the tug of soft pelt, quick cuts, each joint giving way under the knife, her blood soaked hands cleansed by lemon. All the cooking in one pot, herbs, and water, onion tears, green pepper, bones bumping bones, the wild taste of meat changing to something sweet.

AUNT LUCY

She is someone at the end
of a raspy voice,
a handful of tiny bones.
I was a child
when her husband left,
children grew and scattered.
I remember the angry shine
of her kitchen floor,
faded yellow dishes.
I used to hide in her cellar,
among rats and dirty jars.

The years have shaped her
into a hunched shadow,
covered her in dark wool.
When she shakes your hand
she does not let go.
Some nights she cries for her mother.
She wants to be rocked to sleep.
Her hens still lay eggs each day
in old shit and straw.
Soon she will choose the egg
that will be her last meal,
before she breaks open.

FESTA DO ESPIRITO SANTO

Maria Silveira
studies the stained glass,
the lambs and saints.
She kneels and bows,
the host fusing to her tongue
the holiness of her sex,
a scent of blossoms.

A day to be the heroine,
to be the Queen, St. Isabel.
Curls wound from rags cascade her back.
A mother-of-pearl crucifix from *avo*,
the long gown of satin and crocheted
lace from her mother's garment bag.
Beneath her dress, a field of flowers.

She glides down the aisle and onto the street,
a halo of glittering crown and velvet cape.
Side maids and sign bearers,
little queens wrapped in frothy lace
with missing front teeth flank her.
Along the boulevard they float
like angels without bodies
who wear white dresses.

Sweet seller ladies of the Altar Society
offer malasadas, plump and sugared.
Women balance baskets of sweet bread
and sway to the music of the brass band.
Then come the sopas,
a feast for all, of mint flavored stew
with meat that falls easily off the bone.

Find the little queen
tired from standing-very-still
or a slow moving-forward,
asleep in her mother's arms
shadow of halo above her crown.

THEY MEET AT A CHAMARITA

The port, dark and sweet, the swirling light of dance,
his loosened damp collar, her gray skirts, unfolding.
Wrists and hands, the need to touch.
The room rises and falls with their hastening breath.

Spring clutches the plum blossom,
the girl leaves her family for the marriage bed.
Behind pulled curtains,
he watches her undress, her body edged in darkness.
They breathe in the night fragrance of spruce and pine,
wild lupine.
Through half-shut eyes, she is calm and does not speak.

Under his hands, her heart,
like a bird's muffled flutter.
Skin hums, and slender thighs press closer.
Shadows walk above their heads.
They rustle and toss,
till light seeps through the window.
Still, they linger on the paling sheets,
halfway familiar, halfway strange.

THE RANCHER'S WIFE

She raises the shades to dark trees
and glowing fields of wheat and hay.
She opens windows
to the fragrance of honeysuckle,
the sharp smell of manure.

Through the kitchen pane
she watches as his calloused hands
lift bales of hay into air.
She opens the screen door,
and puts her hands in his.
She pulls him inside.

She undresses for him,
rolls her nylons down around her ankles,
removes heart-shaped lace and girdle,
shows him her olive thighs.

She rubs oil in his cracked palms,
removes splinters,
then waits for whatever
his hands will give her.

All night they turn and toss
under a yellow lamp.
At 6:00AM she's calm and slow,
lighting the woodstove
measuring the pour of milk,
the breakfast, ready to serve him.

PEACH CANNING

Under the kitchen faucet my mother scrubs the fur, pulls back the skin. The fruit is picked before ripeness takes hold. The knife my mother uses is the knife her mother used, and is kept sharp for me. She splits golden globes into halves, pulls away the pit, exposes the aching, venous hole.

My father sits on a tree stump and waits for a son to be born. I'm in overalls and boys' shoes, poking a stick in dirt. We eat peaches all year long. In jars the fetal curve of slices float in a clear, thick soup. A white glob of paraffin seals off the air.

UNCLE ERNIE TRIES TO SHOOT ME A PET BIRD

On my fifth birthday,
he's a cowboy,
the birds are the Indians.
Short and beefy with a beard
He wears his Stetson
to look taller.

He fires his shotgun and sound scatters the air.
Sparrows and finches flap from branches,
twigs snap.
I scurry to find a live one,
my fingers sticky with blood and feathers.
Uncle Ernie tells me to look for a linnet
they make good pets
when they're not dead.

By the time the sun is over our heads,
birds decorate the ground.
Uncle Ernie says he will find me a lizard instead.
Says birds are no good anyway,
they eat the fruit off trees.

I want a bird, not a lizard.
After lunch he mixes cherry kool-aide with whiskey.
We watch hummingbirds spin and whirl
till meat bees chase us indoors.
The next day Uncle Ernie buys me a parakeet.

IN THE STARS

My house razed
I live in a modular now,
furnished
and sealed shut.
I won't cook electric
the food tastes flat.

When I get hungry
I build a fire outdoors.
Near the shell of my old house
I cook myself a big pot of beans.
The smell of wood and fresh air
gives the food flavor.

My daughter visits
with the Fire Marshall.
She says if I don't stop
cooking outside,
she will put me in a home.
My home is gone, I say.

I miss the music of the old country—
goats bleating, roosters crowing,
the sound of church bells.
From my casa rustica you could hear
seals bark,
and waves crash against rocks.

At night I look for signs
in the stars,
and see canvas sails of my younger years
billow along routes
the fishing boats took
when they cast-off.

CALIFORNIA TURNING

Winter blackbirds sweep over yellow fields,
with their wings brush over this leaf-sunk November day.
Earth retreats, air turns darker.

By the black strip of highway
a cow's big head hangs over barbed wire.
A horse whinnies in the corral, gallops toward the barn.

Above parched ridges Raven appears—
the Prophet of Winter with black beaked oaths—
shudders snow off pine trees.

Rain charges creeks and streams
skittering like white tailed deer.
Night pulls her in where she dreams and shivers.

Hail unearths rocks.
A broken wing inside her,
and a thousand miles south.

MERCADO

Tied up chickens pile in a heap,
their heads stretch and twitch.
The butcher sharpens his blades.

In the next booth,
a man cuts off a snapper's head,
flings out the guts with his knife,
bundles the body in newspaper.

I hurry past looking for those paper maiche masks,
see an ex-boyfriend in the face of a hairless dog.
For 127 pesos I own his soul.

That night sleep comes in damp, bleached sheets.
I travel with fish in dark caves.

Back on land,
two dogs sniff tails.
One dog grabs me around the ankle,
with his teeth.

Don't feed the pigeons,
they eat meat now.

I wake up in time
to catch a rooster climbing into bed with me.

MUSHROOM WOODS

Evergreen forests
offer their living leaves
while below the surface of this world
mushrooms hide,
wait for the right moment.
A cold dry season
then warm winds, rains
bring forth mycelium masses
that rise up to claim the forest floor.
In darkened thickets
where leaf mat covers ground
they thrust upward,
push through leaves and soil,
explode into moist clumps
to spread spores, seed-like hopes
of future species—
Red Russulas with chalk-white stripes
and spongy brown *Boletus*.
Yellow globe of *Witch's Butter*,
the faint lavender of *Blewitts*.
Slice a red-pored *Bolete*
and its flesh turns blue.
There is risk in naming,
danger in misnaming,
and a short time
to hunt them
before the first frost

IN THE WOODS AT NIGHT

Shadows move in
light falls to the ground.
Colors fill up the darkness
clots of red, spasms of purple.
My eyesight dims.
Deer trail sinks into canyon.

When night comes alive
it hums, it crawls.
I can hear the deep dead turn,
see dirt bulge with roots.
Eyes shine on me
a wet nose touches my hand.

Unwinged, human
I want to save myself from danger
but with no sharp beak or claws
I can't protect myself
from hungry raptors
a world that gets up on all fours.

COILED SPRING

The girl walks out over
the frozen landscape,
follows a trail into the woods.

Twilight and mist spread into darkness
and her feet cannot find the way back.

Hungry, she eats red berries
without thinking of Persephone.

A voice deep under leaves
calls to her, the earth opens beneath her feet.

She breathes in a scent of musk,
finds herself face to face with Hades.

She's led through a labyrinth of time,
where past and future lose shape,
where the dead eat the living,
not for hunger,
but to taste the sun
they will never see.

Crowned, *Queen of Seeds*,
and condemned to a longing for light,
she dreams the passage
of one season to the next,
her heart sprouting a green thread.

She unknots her roots,
twists and pulls loose
from the hard ground.

Her soul, a coiled embryo
trembling into brightness.

THE WIDOW SILVA

She buried his ashes
then planted a tree in them.
Nights she sleeps on a cold mattress.

Today she sits on the porch
in her new chair from Sears
peeling apples.

Her husband's old mare
leans against the fence
heaves and coughs,
nose in the dirt.

She pushes against gravity
rises from her rocker.

Gray Sally follows her easy,
limps out to pasture
trails her along the cow path.

Eyes sharp and wild,
the crack of a rifle.
The widow leaves the mare
where she falls.
Leaves her for the wolves.

Back at home,
the apples are turning brown.
And it's time to take corn to the hens,
turn the bull out to the cows,
check for leaning fences.

CROW CROSSING

The crow flies
out of tree shade.

The sun sifts through clouds,
pours itself over the bird.

Like a streak of blurred charcoal,
the bird leaves his shining behind,

moves from brightness
to his usual dark self.

Suddenly the air darkens
like a fire taking flight.

The moon squeezes
between two branches.

Wings cover the sky.

WHAT MATTERS IN THE MORNING

when light fills my window,
and overflows the sun across my bed,
I watch the mountains move closer,
coming home with the daylight.
A monarch flutters into the garden,
rests on a hollyhock,
peacefully opens its wings.
I see something shimmer
between the corn rows.
It's my father in old shoes and coveralls
hoeing, tracking weeds along snail roads,
standing up straight, head bent and focused
on the endless furrows of his eighty six years.
The sun shines greenly on his hands
as he listens to roots inch deeper into earth,
watches baby spiders hatch, flex their legs.
When he sees me at the window
I hold my hand up to wave,
he holds his,
we are palm to palm.

SAVING MYSELF

My ancestors are stones in the river.
They sparkle,
their quartz veins
glisten in granite.
I wade carefully,
feeling with bare feet
smooth skinned stones.
A muskrat swims by me
slick-backed, fur shining.

Braced against current
and slippery bank
I lose my step,
I fall into the cold stream.
A water sprite travels
1000 years
to swim through my bones.
Minnows scatter;
I drink the river.

Deer breathe hard in the shadows.
In the pines a spotted owl chants,
and an old, scaly fish
beats up from the bottom,
then sinks back down again.

I rise from the current,
find shallow water,
sit among the stones.
In a mountain pool
where a trout darts,
I bless my reflection.

PART TWO

The dead pass quickly. They cannot be held on to.
As soon as one leaves, another one's tapping
your shoulder.

—Carlos Drummond De Andrade

DON'T SCORN THE DEAD WHO ARE OURSELVES

Nights I wait for signs of her coming,
a face in half-light, pale tissue of heartbeat.
Perhaps the orb moving past me in the hallway,
the air scented with the dying curl of Jasmine.

I wait for the clock to fall exhausted into dream state,
finally close my eyes in sleep.
A hole of light pours through the ceiling,
and my future visits me, a specter
in a grainy black and white vision.

I stare into her phantom face,
and see myself as I will be.
She slumps into my arms like a limp pieta,
body translucent, cool to touch.
I spread my arms open,
and fall awake.

Years ahead of us move in parallel worlds,
never touching.
Someday, not yet, a crossing over.

AT THE MORTUARY

Times of sorrow,
and times of relief,

heated death rooms
of the elders' eternal bulk
sits me down.

I don't move,
and become their monument.

On the mahogany table
a pot of cold tea;
overripe fruit fills the compote dish.

Candles open coffin eyes.
There comes a muttering,
and the dead pull away from their bodies.

White, waving curtains
scatter flecks of soot
like moths.

With a sudden tearing of wind,
still windows fly open
to breathe again.

THE OLD WOMAN'S LAST DAYS

The people stop on the rocky hilltop, look out at the world, watch it wane. The land drained of color, of life, the hills gray. Below them the rust-stained valley, the smell of spilled oil lingers in the air. The brown snaking river the only thing to follow. The old woman leads their way, walking days of weary distances toward mountains. They don't hear the footsteps behind them, or see human faces forming from the granite rock. Scattered by the fright of sudden movement, a flock of birds flies off.

The people make camp, build a fire. The old woman gathers fistfuls of twigs, throws her arms into the fossil moon. She stamps the ground makes small cracks appear. Her long white hair floats as she turns and spins, blurring the world around her. She needs to believe in a place beyond her mind, what her heart finds when she closes her eyes. Inside her skull, oceans and continents, forests and plains.

Men in camouflage hunt the people down. They say the old woman is a deer. They eat her.

FOLKLORE

If only we understood the story about the woodsman and his children. Why the wind plays music through dry grass and deer move toward the lowlands. Everything blurring. Procession of dark shadows running. The trees, the smoke, the flames, firemen sunk to their knees.

Tinged by blaze the timber wolf takes a human voice, crouches for cover, yowls for help. We follow the trail of bright trees, twist into hot coils air rushing out of body. Some of us fly, sharp bones turning into wings, heaviness becoming the lightest of moments.

Like Hansel and Gretel here in the forest, in the fire, we hear the witch laugh in the crackling night.

BONE HUNTING IN THE SIERRAS

High on an open ridge,
overlooking mountains and valleys
I hunger for a history deep underground,
the marrow of before-hand.

A mountain's wind rage
pelts dust in my face,
fills me with earth,
searches me for bones and fossils.

Shadows shift,
and a Red-Tail
without moving a wing
floats above.

Tracks in sandstone
my fingertips trace,
find missing vertebrae and skull,
ease into a kinship with a broken pelvis.

Rocks unfold themselves into arms and legs.
I push root-limbs
back inside the hard mountain
toward the deepness, the origin of all things.

Scream of hawk,
slow grind of bedrock,
that deep down ache
as pieces of myself fall away

FISHERMAN AT EAGLE LAKE, CALIFORNIA

Up to his thighs,
he pulls fish from the dark lake,
brings them to the light to die,
nothing slips away.
Some he jerks out of the shallows,
too small, so he throws them back.
Crazed for water,
big fish from the deep
wiggle and twist,
gulp air through their gills.
He cuts off heads,
splits them gullet to tail,
yanks out the life strings,
scrapes scales to skin.
He tosses the innards into the water.
What he leaves behind will meet the surface
like a bubble of air.
Lemon, sliced down the center,
washed over palms,
between fingers, over wrists.
And now the smell of death is hidden,
like the jacket of the lost boy
last seen across the lake crying.

QUERCUS

The Live Oak—
full, and fluttering.

One muscled arm,
crooked around the sun.

Through woody lifelines
stubby fingers

reach up and out,
grab at rushing clouds.

Breezes bury me with branches,
dark seeds enter my flesh.

I see with my fingertips,
draw out my own world.

Sunlight burns leaves into birds,
whirled into sky.

RIVER IN THE ROAD

A flood of stillness
    widens the road,
        covers the solid line.

People in rubber boots
    move along the shoulder,
        spilling their identities.

The missing,
    a river of pulse beats
        weighted down by debris.

When full morning comes
    water opens like a gill,
        a salmon shoots into sunlight.

Road crews wake up,
    find rats and men
        living together in storm drains.

A woman leans into the street,
    her face a blossom
        falling to the water's surface.

APPROACHING THE LAST SEASON

Time to live with wings.
Tips pierce her skin, she bleeds.

Moon fills the room with primal shining
as dying stars rest on her breasts.

She's half dressed,
head tucked under a pinion.

In a breeze her future
passes through the window.

Flutter of trapped wing beats
in her rib cage.

The hand inside herself
reaches out,

plucks her from the earth,
tosses her into sky.

THE SURGE

In this season of dry leaves,
the girl searches for the promise of a future
in the shine, the pulse of a mountain stream.

She hears splashing.
Through spread of oak and alder,
sees the surge of salmon.

The air sweet and fetid
with fish odor.
In pools the males dart and recoil,
the females quiet with birth pulse.

Thrash of fin, twist of body,
soft spill of eggs,
sky immerses itself in water.

Soon they will be dead,
bodies of ragged flesh battered
by their passion.

She stands on stones in the whirling wash,
rescues a tattered female afloat on the current,
blows into its mouth,
places it in the shallows,
moves it back and forth,
forces water between its jaws.

But the salmon belongs to the creek.

Stepping into the cold flow,
lunging forward, she wills herself back
to the source.

THE SHAPE OF GRIEF

The chime at midnight curves around the open wound of her grief. Moths visit this sleepless night when pain forces her to turn on the light. Dazzled by the glow, she watches their shadows flutter across the frost wrapped window. She wants something to hurt outside herself.

The night is long, and for hours she listens to beating wings against glittering glass. They will die from the freeze. In the morning their bodies, wings spread open like hands in the ice, stuck on brick work.

She lies under the ceiling bulb. A gypsy moth grows inside her chest, replaces her shrinking heart.

TRANSPARENT SPHERE

I greet them at the front door, shivering and skeletal, light too bright to bear, no shadows anywhere. Death has softened the lines in their faces, transformed the bitterness of dying memory into something bittersweet. Behind them the bare Oak looms, branching in all directions, from life to life, what my flesh is heir to. They walk into my house pulling the past into the present.

I say, "You can't come back, you can't come back and haunt me."

Snow in my heart, snow in my eyes. They live now in a snow globe on the mantel, placed safely among mountains rounded.

POPPY SEEDS ON STONES

Nights I can't sleep,
I rescue moths.
They flop around my lantern.
I gather them in a tablecloth,
and watch them flutter toward the moon.
The ones I can't save,
litter the porch like leaves.

This morning I cross the cemetery
and find my family plot.
I place poppy seeds on the stones,
the shadow of a hawk
rumples over the grass.

Clouds are pulled apart
by the wind—
there is something about
their torn white mouths,
separated like the dead
who will one day take
my hands as I rise,
the mirage of a wave
off a hot field.

PRAY, SING

1

The California Condor circles on wind trails
knows to find its center.

Two elk disappear into tree line,
moss deep.

The sound of hoof beat,
my body startled, watchful.

Things gone under the surface.
Flesh of caves, old lava tubes cool and hollow.

Stones in the earth rattle.

I pray, I sing, I listen.

2

The Condor imagines
me caught at last in his beak.

At the edge
sunlight traces pathways.

The spiral down,
my center weightless.

I run into afterlife,
death so warm it beats like a heart.

Wing clap.

The leap, the lift,
the falling of feathers.

GRANDFATHER

You go during one winter.
The years have flattened your grave with the earth,
wind wiped your name from the granite stone.

You had woods and weather,
rising bluffs and arching sky,
mountains that lift clear to the ocean.
The apple orchard you set on the green hill.
Sons and daughters all born
in your old mountain home.

You worked year after year,
plowing back and forth with your shaggy-maned horse,
clans of birds, tribes of beasts in the forest.
I can see you working cattle since daybreak
then home by nightfall, for supper and sleep.

No tree, or stone, or fence, the same,
since you left.
The brown barn leans like an animal,
the apples are small and bitter.
Hungry deer straggle in leaving bits of hide
on barbed wire.

I remember your promise of a hike in the woods,
a swim in the pond, the trout we might catch.
In dreams, you tell me to rake the dead stalks,
clean the earth bare again, scatter the wild grass.

THE CROSSING

No one walks the cattle path now, no one but the cows.
I follow tracks deep in the ground, sink into spring ooze
where several layers down
lie those who cultivated this land.
In the soft ticking of weeds
I hear singing,
harmonies I do not understand.
The wind hisses the names of the dead,
and from a clover bed, without wings or halos,
they rise up to walk the pasture.

When a hawk drifts down, hooked claws extended,
my feet crush lupines and buttercups.
I run toward Moffett Road.
From an oak a shadow of birds explodes,
and the air hums with souls.
No breath
I reach paved road and walk toward town.
Ranchers wave when I pass
as though I have forgotten something,
as though I should turn back.

LAST OF HER LINE

She follows ghost ruts of extinct wagon roads,
finds her husband, her mother, her baby.
They make their way single file
along the night trails of her memory.

Bent to the ground with age,
with the death of everyone she knows,
she walks slowly over the pasture.
Near a stand of oaks
through vein work of branches,
the sky signals to her eyes.

In a field wrapped by barbed wire
where death perches on fence posts
she goes down on her knees
with wild mustard and gopher holes.

The snake tenses its body
as she waits,
on the other side of cold grasses.

SHE ENTERS AN INUIT WORLD

She escapes into the wild to get away from people. The animal inside gnaws her ribs to free itself, as the mountain rises off its haunches, and thunder growls in greeting. Ache of bone, marrow of memory, pain cleaves, pulls her into the primal gene pool.

In sleep she dreams of finding eggs in high grass. At midnight the moon devours the mountain raw. The sky holds stars of animal skulls, skeletons of old friends. The savage of her heart wakes. The buck tilts its rack, and she's at his throat.

She lives for flesh off the bone. With only spirits in a soup pot, she wakes each morning hungry. In the meadow she's on heels and paws, wrapped in pelts, her knapsack stuffed with animal tracks, crouched over old bones, mud, and ash.

Darkness gathers in the grass. The wind blows dust, turns the landscape imaginary, a doe invisible. The sun leaps from the paws of a mountain lion, its warm mouth on her neck. As the cat's grip tightens, she looks up at herself in the sky.

FINDING THE SACRED

Born with question marks
about my past,
my people,
I step inside myself
and find running water,
stones too heavy to bring up.
These waters fill the banks
with gold dust and granite,
shining mica and quartz.
No heaven here, but root,
alluvial and veined.
Still I hear voices,
see ghosts drift in and out,
the drone of the river.

In the old growth forest
I listen for footsteps,
and hear birdsong.
In this place of rest,
this ancestral path of migration,
the air pulses angelic
from the throat of a sparrow.
In my hands, the smell of prayer
gathered in a lavender bouquet.
Madrone bark,
red and gold,
flames like candles.
Crows on the church roof
a choir of ancestors chanting.

PART THREE

INITIAL

The sea blue and white and the gleaming
Stones — the breathless space
Where what is cleansed re-cleanses
For the rite of awe and commencement
Where I am to myself given back
In salt, foam and shell returned
To the initial beach of my life.

—Sophia de Mello Breyner Andresen

LOST CURRENTS

The sea, the sky,
the birthright of her being.
Stones that sound against water,
against stone, heart of stone.
How deep the stone's truth.

The passion of a rising tide,
wave, after wave,
of memory.
Dream eye of wave,
fish eye.

Her people mapping sea routes.
De Gama rounding the Cape
of Good Hope.
Lost, in the folds of dark sea,
exile of spirit.

Salt, the skin
of another life.
A thousand histories,
charts, scaled and starry,
to steer by.

FESTO DO EMIGRANTE

They sense the coast near,
hear the foghorn's incantation.
They have crossed the great ocean,
their silver hair blowing in the wind.

Voices pulse through the air,
some speaking American.
At first just a mist, a slight drizzle,
primes their memory,
of waters where their fathers fished.

Forty years gone
till the waves bring them home.
They move down the gangplank,
some smile and carry gifts,
others, heads down, empty handed.

Those on shore don't remember names.
One man throws his arms
around his mother's neck.
She slips his grasp,
believing him a ghost.

They go back down the road
the way they came.
Here is home, they say.

THE ASSUMPTION

In the cave of rocks the forgotten statue
trembles in high winds.
Rushing, roiling waters
loosen all her bonds.

The plastic Madonna, she slides
then somersaults beneath the surface,
tossed from swell to swell,
rising, falling, resurging.

She's exposed, immortal,
burdened with the weight of Ascension,
the physics of longing
for the world promised.

Touched by the sun,
she finds herself in a congregation of clouds.
Among cumulus she looks for her son.

When the tides turn back,
her feet barely touch the tops of waves.

BOUND

I found a ship bound for the old country, so I could travel back to a past I never lived, to the life of my great grandmother, the woman who started my story... I twisted her ring on my finger, and made a wish. At the altar I kneeled for prayer and host, asked for the body and blood, asked for the resurrection of her body. I wanted her whole again, so we could find our way back together.

Crocheted into the night my *bisavo* talked to me in my language that she couldn't understand. She told me she wanted to go home. A ghost ship docked. It sat silent in the black water and waited for us to board. Her body merged with mine. We returned.

The island she remembered was dressed in crags and calderas. She said to me in broken English that when the lava stopped boiling, fish came to the shore and begged to be caught. Her hand filled with sky, breakers flowered on the beach, stones showed their frowning faces. She helped me understand the waves, close and far. Showed me how to pass through air, pass through water, enter salt.

THE PULL OF WATER

Convulsion of island flesh,
soar of ash settles into cloud,
the crumble at the edge of all they know.

Tumbling into the sea,
they struggle to keep afloat,
their exhausted breath, the letting go.

The sea swells, bursts open.
Currents, gravity, wind, call their fate.
The surface keeps breaking, the sky keeps moving.
They drift further away from home,
breathe the ocean in unison.

She dreams between black rocks,
listens to water tell stories of her ancestors.
In her mind she reaches out her hand
to meet them in a new world,
as they climb out of the ocean.

Give her sleep, let her find herself restored,
reunited with who she is,
where she came from.

Before morning she'll swim back to earth,
her body growing heavy.
The sunrise like giant wings flies upward,
a voice and a hand on her shoulder.

PENANCE

The priest's parish totters on the precipice where he waits for his lost congregation at a makeshift altar. Inside the caldera a green flesh of garden. Hundreds of feet down, the baptismal font, where lie bones of saints, and drowned sinners. On the rim the priest survives, lives with what he has. Had he been a bird he would fly, beat air into holy water. He sags under the weight of the dead gull he may have rescued, or killed, lying limp on his shoulder. On the bird's neck, flattened feathers. The priest loosens his collar, reaches for a rock against which his suffering falls.

FLORES ISLAND

The place at the beginning

A whale rises up in her mind
turning her thoughts gray.

In port, the ferry of return.
She searches for her grandfather
to discover the shape of his emigration
and finds the plank's gone, rotted.
At the mercy of rough water and high winds,
he rowed, sinews pulling his dory,
pulling his bones to breaking.

She scans the distance,
says his name out loud, *Antonio Henriques*,
waits to hear a voice, see a face.
She searches for all the prisoners
of thick mists, others who look like her,
whose foreign tongues speak music to her soul.

Beyond the wake of a rogue wave,
currents and tides ride
on the back of a gray whale.

She sees through the vapor
boats whose nets gather the sky and let go.
Fog falls,
bearing dazed souls back to their home place.
She falls with them.

AT THE VILLAGE OF SANTA BARBARA, ISLAND OF PICO

Looking for my great, great grandmother, Maria Francesca do Cabral

My fingernails scraped lava stones,
loosened dust.

Looking for the other world
I found a fissure in the earth that led
to where the sea tossed its wet creatures,
their lungs exhaling.

The ocean spread dark and cold beneath the night,
reached with every wave
for drops of light shed by the moon.

Musty air and a ghost rattle through banana leaves
you rose up, bones of family architecture, luminous.
A woman without soil, you carved roots
from stones of the island.

Into the Azorean sea you dove.
The splash of your body, and I jumped,
scattering stars, to pull toward you.
Where ocean and sky met, you vanished.

Your memory, the afterlife dissolving
all that salt
seeped back into the sea
an ocean mist without end.

I held my breath, heard the heartbeat of waves,
felt the ocean of my blood.
My body took pleasure in forgetting gravity,
the need for breathing on my own.

I asked God to throw me a line.
Floating to the shore I felt the pull of the universe
slow everything down, as heaven pulled the earth
into its arms.

SOUL OF BLACK STONE,

Ilha das Flores

On the black beach, the mystery.
She talks to dark stones,
knows them.

With the new moon,
voices familiar, call to her.
She can't make out what they say,

she above them,
like a wave falling
when the tide turns.

Her people, most at home in the sea.
The body of water from where they came,
her same blood.

She wants to study the currents,
swim in them, surf their waves,
taste of their salt.

FLORES ISLAND, THE AZORES, 2008

She walks a footpath,
comes upon native species,
finds restless slopes.

On the hillside
veined with blue, floral hedges,
a sting of mint in the air.

Rain she senses
at the edges of her thoughts,
weighs clouds down.

Rainwater turns to mist, to air,
to time passing,
days, years, this moment.

She catches the glint in a rabbit's eye.
A spiral of vapor, ghostlike,
vanishes among crags.

The caldera's green eye stares,
watches her lose herself
in a waterfall.

She plunges,
wanting to see how far she can go,
wanting the shock of going under.

DREAMING VULCAN

Land and sea converge where she finds a deep island, seismic and sated with ghostly geography of rocks, crevasses, rucked earth. Ancient buildings collapse. The dark Cathedral folds into itself, bells swing, haloed heads and winged shoulders crumble. Birds shriek, and feathers of fire break into flight.

Everything she touches burns. Her breath flares, flames, speak for her in a dead language. The earth roars and heaves, she clings to the tops of boulders, then falls like lava or water over rock into deep surf, lets the drift flow inside and outside herself. Island at her back, she swims toward open sea, into the here and now, soul tossed and speechless.

WHAT THE TIDE BRINGS IN

The tide comes in like my white bearded ancestors. Waves strike me down, hissing salt water, and I hear my dead grandmother calling. The muscle of tide holds me, then drags me to shore over rocks and shells. I lie here, bruised from the struggles in my life, and years away from my grandmother's tender reach. My self freed, lifted whole from the sea, washed up to lie on rocks, to watch the turning back of tides and their return.

I rise to see a creature tangled in fish net, flippers, fin-thin, flailing, dragging on the beach toward me. I turn the creature on its back, its yellow-green underbelly wet and soft, its flippers drooping over the edge of its shell. It lies still as I untangle it. Once freed from the netting, I flip it back over. Right side up again the reptile stares at me with its prehistoric eyes. Revived, it makes a dash toward the sea where it evolved from egg to lizard. Hard shell afloat it skims the surface beaked head darting, its torso rocking against the rhythm of the current. The brine sloshes against rocks as the creature turns, dives, presses its body farther into the sea, hauled by the tides, to come into, out of, and finally under.

THE WHITE CITY

Above seven hills the sol star shines,
casts away shadow.
Wind carries time around, and past,
raises up dust.

When white Freesia leans
against stained glass,
the fadista sweeps heat
down the boulevards.

A glow seizes albescent patinas,
as specters buff the domed church,
and ethers rise up with fish-eyes.

The Tagus River brings home the lost ones
through wrack, and conch,
messages of salt.

On the Avenida da Liberdade,
people call out for Santo Antonio,
discover lost things.

Find the Madonna down a quiet alley.
She stands on a gate,
uses aquamarines to cut the air,
then hems the sky with gold thread.

THE SWALLOWS RETURN TO LISBON

They return to the eaves of their birth,
collective memory, an omen of better days
to welcome warmer weather.

Crosses of light in the sky,
they bring messages from the dead,
returning to the ritual of grief,
to what is lost, memories of each spring.

Hope has heavy doors,
and the flock circles the ancient cathedral
where hungry people live,
fed by wine and bread.

In uncertain spaces they unfold
the dream of feathers.
From bell towers, wings rise,
music reaching out to the Tagus.

The one chosen
to carry the sorrows of the world away
beats its wings.

SÉ DE LISBOA, JULY 2011

She has travelled the long distance
without gifts, and no star to follow.
Inside, saints open and close doors,

wavering light slants
through the rose window,
falls to the floor.

The smell of incense, the touch of holy water,
and she can't stop her inner trembling.

In St. Vincent's Chapel,
two ancient ravens
hold the black of deepest ocean.

In the sanctuary she turns her back
to dying candles, crosses empty rows.

The air is heavy.
Prayers travel upward,
then plummet back down again.

She wants the bread, the wine,
the miracles.

At the altar she sees the pale face of Jesus
among bruised lilies,
and knows there's no end to falling.

A ONE BREASTED WOMAN DRESSED IN A SHROUD

She doesn't notice the dark forces
lurking in her body,
until the excision of her right breast.

Now, crows pour out of her,
hands at the tips of their pinions.
They writhe on the floor beside her bed.

The skin in her chest burns.
She's not a bird,
not even a woman.

She bathes in the dark,
covers her red slash
with linens.

One shoulder sinks into her heart,
her pulse becomes a flapping wing,
a noose holds up her right arm.

See her like Saint Agatha,
with a dove on her shoulder,
carrying her breast on a silver plate.

THE BIRD INSIDE HER HEAD

A darkness shoots through the window.
She chases it with a broom,
screams, sweeps the air.
A feathered creature squawks back at her.

Flailing, flapping wings
rising and falling,
Bird darkness assaults her,
a windfall of feathers.

Like a dust devil it whirls close to her face,
enters her ear canal.
She feels a flutter inside her head.

Avernal toxins rise,
and her mind grows wings.
Memories, fevers, swirl,
her lips blow feathers,
her heart, a blister throbbing.

In her room the curtains hang like empty sleeves.
The window opens and a bird flies out.

A SEASHELL MYTHOLOGY

Light from the window falls in blue pools on the floor.
The room becomes an ocean.
Waves lift and drop her till she's worn away,
and sharp edges turn smooth.

Time changes its course, and the past traps her in its nets.
Her mother snorkels past, silver-fin moving,
her father on a rock poised for a dive.
Hands cupped she reaches toward shore.

Around her neck, grandma Mary's gold crucifix
weighs her down.
Salt water fills nostrils, seeps into her soul.
On the beach the tide finds her curled inside a shell hiding.

WITCH OF FLORES ISLAND

Into the bubbling caldera,
the witch flings basalt,
fills her pockets with bones and ash.

Sun and moon avoid her—
she reaches high to grab the lunar disc,
but it slips her grasp.
The sol star coats her with salt.

She's a hunched sorceress who lost her powers,
image thrown back by her silver mirror.
No more eyes or hands conjuring fishermen
to wait for her onshore.

A crone, blistered and dry,
face more carapace than flesh,
talks in a language of dark, mean stones.

Splash into ocean waters,
for baptism of a born again witch,
the Atlantic flows in and out of her.
She chokes, coughs lava,

swims to the place
where the ships went down,
slips into fog.

Find her now,
smoke rising from a cluster of Hydrangeas,
conjuring a new life—
hair dyed henna, nails polished red.

WHERE THE LIONESS GOES

When the savage goddess within her
wakes in the night,
her dreams spill into her mouth,
slip over teeth and tongue,
taste of blood.

Her roar scatters stars and wolves,
as she stalks a deeper world.
In her life she ran a long way,
pack at her heels,
hunters not far behind.

She drinks at the river,
finds a woman's face staring back,
all fours changing to hands and knees,
wild blood,
feline strong.

THE HIGH WINDS

She resists.
  The gale
shakes her house,
  and sets loose lawn chairs.
They sail
  across the yard.
Stars capsize
  through trees.
Newspapers flap
  open,
and rustle down the road.
  Under a sky
full of falling
  she thinks
she's safe inside.
  The storm mocks her,
and searches out
  each crack,
presses against
  each pane of glass,
tells her
  how thin
the walls.
  In the morning
she wakes
  with a clear mind
to pure space,
  and promises
to live
  with whatever the wind
gives her.

KISSING THE BEE

She waits for the slow sun,
the long pull from the earth
after rain.

Sunlight passes through her.
Glands turn to pollen.

From the bed she rises,
legs hung deep in darkness.

The sudden burst of seedpod
and leaves sprout from her ribs.

She opens in a whorl of bloom,
smear of color.

Her body a busy, dark flower.

Her center attracts the bee
who wiggles itself
into her sticky womb.

They embrace,
till longing turns to dust.

WOMAN OF THE ROWAN

In Norse mythology the rowan is known as the tree from which the first woman was made

The first woman picks up bones of wood on the forest floor.
A gloomy rain dies before touching the ground,
like bitter tears.

When lightning strikes her down,
a shriek, and her eyes close,
her heart goes to sleep.

In the darkness of fallen logs and moss,
oaks circle her—
they lift her, carry her through the woodland.

She's passed from branch to branch,
planted in the sediments,
kneaded into tree shape.

She grows upward, springs through herself
till she stands tall before the world.
Rooted to soil, she holds her arms aloft and crooked.

Each day the wind, the rotting leaves.
From his cave, the bear rises with his hungry teeth.
Mud and rain radiate through trees.

The seasons know when to leave, when to come.
When spring sun filters through her crown,
the earth blooms woman again.

With a forked branch she searches for memory,
finds the bones of wood she once came from,
crumbled, turned to dust.

LET HER BE A FLOWER

Let her musk bouquet rise,
and the bee crawl into her helix,
all honeyed and pleasured.

Fill her with longing,
and sweet clover dreams.
Give her the appetite of a queen.

Let her colors show,
till night lay down in the meadow.

In August when she burns
let her blood and seed
leach into dark soil.

NOTES ON THE TEXT

Page 18, 23: "Chamarita" is a popular folk dance originating from the Azores in Portugal.

Page 22: "*avo*" is the Portuguese word for grandmother and "Festa do Espirito Santo" or feast of the Holy Spirit. Festa do Espirito Santo is the Azorean American Holy Ghost Festival held between Easter and late fall. The festa honors the memory of 14th century Queen Isabel, a peacemaker and friend to the poor. The Portuguese believe that the Holy Spirit enabled Isabel to relieve her people's suffering. According to legend, the queen, while smuggling food to the poor in midwinter, produced live roses from her robes when her husband, King Dom Diniz, demanded to see what she was concealing. There are also other versions of this legend.

Page 27: "Casa rustica" is a rustic house

Page 29: "Mercado" is the Spanish word for market.

Page 45: "Quercus" is an oak tree.

Page 62: "Festo do Emigrante" On Flores Island in the Azores, the Emigrant Festival is the largest city festival, where history, culture, and traditions are celebrated in programs that include traditional music and dance.

Page 64: "bisavo" translates to mean great grandmother in Portuguese.

Page 67: "Flores Island" is one of nine volcanic islands in the North Atlantic Ocean that together make up what is known as the Azores.

Page 66: "caldera" is a large volcanic crater

Page 69: "Ilha dos Flores" or Island of Flores in the Azores

Page 73: "The White City" references Lisbon which is sometimes called "The White City." "Freesia" is a type of flower. "Fadista" is that person who sings Fado music. "Domed Church" refers to the Lisbon Cathedral. "Tagus River" is the longest river on the Iberian Peninsula and flows through Lisbon where it empties into the Atlantic. "Avenida do Liberdade" is a celebrated avenue in central Lisbon. "Santo Antonio" refers to Saint Anthony the patron saint of Portugal.

Page 75: "Sé De Lisboa" refers to the Lisbon Cathedral that was said to have been built in the year 1150. "St. Vincent" is considered the patron saint of Lisbon.

Page 76: "Saint Agatha" is a martyr. One of the tortures she allegedly suffered was having her breasts cut off, and is often portrayed carrying her breasts on a plate.

ABOUT THE AUTHOR

Lara Gularte lives and writes in the Sierra foothills of California. She was featured in the Autumn 2014 (vol. 20, no. 2) issue of *The Bitter Oleander.* Her poetry, depicting her Azorean heritage, is included in a book of essays called "Imaginários Luso-Americanos e Açorianos" by Vamberto Freitas. Additional writings may be found in *The Gávea-Brown Book of Portuguese-American Poetry*, and in *Writers of the Portuguese Diaspora in the United States and Canada.* Gularte earned an MFA degree from San Jose State University where she not only served as a poetry editor for *Reed Magazine,* but received the Anne Lillis Award for Creative Writing, along with several Phelan Awards. Her work has appeared widely in journals and magazines, and has been included in many national and regional anthologies. In 2017 she traveled to Cuba with a delegation of American poets and presented her poetry at the Festival Internacional de Poesia de la Habana.She is currently an assistant editor for *Narrative Magazine.*